Santa
Monica
Public
Library

4-WEEK
LOAN

FOR TELEPHONE RENEWALS CALL:

Main Library 451-1866
Ocean Park Branch 392-3804
Fairview Branch 450-0443
Montana Branch 829-7081

DATE DUE

Symphony No. 4
in E Minor, Op. 98

Johannes Brahms

DOVER PUBLICATIONS, INC.
Mineola, New York

Published in Canada by General Publishing Company, Ltd., 30 Lesmill Road, Don Mills, Toronto, Ontario.
Published in the United Kingdom by Constable and Company, Ltd., 3 The Lanchesters, 162–164 Fulham Palace Road, London W6 9ER.

Bibliographical Note

This Dover edition, first published in 1997, is a republication of music from Volume 1 of "Symphonien für Orchester," edited by Hans Gál, from *Johannes Brahms, Sämtliche Werke / Ausgabe der Gesellschaft der Musikfreunde in Wien*, originally published by Breitkopf & Härtel, Leipzig, n.d.

International Standard Book Number: 0-486-29891-4

Manufactured in the United States of America
Dover Publications, Inc., 31 East 2nd Street, Mineola, N.Y. 11501

CONTENTS

Symphony No. 4
in E Minor, Op. 98

(1885)

INSTRUMENTATION

2 Flutes [Flöten, Fl.]
Flute 2 doubles Piccolo [Kleine Flöte, kl. Fl.]
2 Oboes [Oboen, Ob.]
2 Clarinets in C, A [Klarinetten, Klar.]
2 Bassoons [Fagotte, Fag.]
Contrabassoon [Kontrafagott, K.-Fag.]

4 Horns in C, E, F [Hörner, Hr.]
2 Trumpets in C, E [Trompeten, Trpt.]
3 Trombones [Posaunen, Pos.]

Timpani [Pauken, Pk.]
Triangle [Triangel, Trgl.]

Violins 1, 2 [Violine, Viol.]
Violas [Bratsche, Br.]
Cellos [Violoncell, Vcl.]
Basses [Kontrabaß, K.-B.]

Symphony No. 4
in E Minor, Op. 98

Allegro non troppo

2 Flöten
2 Oboen
Klarinetten in A
2 Fagotte
in E 1.2.
4 Hörner
in C 3.4.
Trompeten in E
Pauken in E u. H
1. Violine
2. Violine
Bratsche
Violoncell
Kontrabaß

Allegro non troppo

7
Fl.
Klar. (A)
Fag.
Hr. 3. (C) 4.
1.Viol.
2.Viol.
Br.
Vcl.
K.-B.

1

2

4

6

8

12

17

26

30

38

Allegro giocoso

Große Flöte

Kleine Flöte

2 Oboen

2 Klarinetten in C

2 Fagotte

Kontrafagott

4 Hörner in F 1. 2.

in C 3. 4.

2 Trompeten in C

Pauken in F G C

Triangel

1.Violine

2.Violine

Bratsche

Violoncell

Kontrabaß

Allegro giocoso

42

46

48

51

54

56

62

68

68

74

80

98

END OF EDITION

DOVER FULL-SIZE
ORCHESTRAL SCORES

THE SIX BRANDENBURG CONCERTOS AND THE FOUR ORCHESTRAL SUITES IN FULL SCORE, Johann Sebastian Bach. Complete standard Bach-Gesellschaft editions in large, clear format. Study score. 273pp. 9 x 12. 23376-6 Pa. **$12.95**

COMPLETE CONCERTI FOR SOLO KEYBOARD AND ORCHESTRA IN FULL SCORE, Johann Sebastian Bach. Bach's seven complete concerti for solo keyboard and orchestra in full score from the authoritative Bach-Gesellschaft edition. 206pp. 9 x 12. 24929-8 Pa. **$11.95**

THE THREE VIOLIN CONCERTI IN FULL SCORE, Johann Sebastian Bach. concerto in A Minor, BWV 1041; Concerto in E Major, BWV 1042; and Concerto for Two Violins in D Minor, BWV 1043. Bach-Gesellschaft edition. 64pp. 9⅜ x 12¼. 25124-1 Pa. **$6.95**

GREAT ORGAN CONCERTI, OPP. 4 & 7, IN FULL SCORE, George Frideric Handel. 12 organ concerti composed by great Baroque master are reproduced in full score from the *Deutsche Handelgesellschaft* edition. 138pp. 9⅜ x 12¼. 24462-8 Pa. **$12.95**

COMPLETE CONCERTI GROSSI IN FULL SCORE, George Frideric Handel. Monumental Opus 6 Concerti Grossi, Opus 3 and "Alexander's Feast" Concerti Grossi—19 in all—reproduced from most authoritative edition. 258pp. 9⅜ x 12¼. 24187-4 Pa. **$13.95**

LATER SYMPHONIES, Wolfgang A. Mozart. Full orchestral scores to last symphonies (Nos. 35–41) reproduced from definitive Breitkopf & Härtel Complete Works edition. Study score. 285pp. 9 x 12. 23052-X Pa. **$14.95**

PIANO CONCERTOS NOS. 17–22, Wolfgang Amadeus Mozart. Six complete piano concertos in full score, with Mozart's own cadenzas for Nos. 17–19. Breitkopf & Härtel edition. Study score. 370pp. 9⅜ x 12¼. 23599-8 Pa. **$16.95**

PIANO CONCERTOS NOS. 23–27, Wolfgang Amadeus Mozart. Mozart's last five piano concertos in full score, plus cadenzas for Nos. 23 and 27, and the Concert Rondo in D Major, K.382. Breitkopf & Härtel edition. Study score. 310pp. 9⅜ x 12¼. 23600-5 Pa. **$16.95**

DAPHNIS AND CHLOE IN FULL SCORE, Maurice Ravel. Definitive full-score edition of Ravel's rich musical settings of a Greek fable by Longus is reprinted here from the original French edition. 320pp. 9⅜ x 12¼. (Not available in France or Germany) 25826-2 Pa. **$17.95**

THREE GREAT ORCHESTRAL WORKS IN FULL SCORE, Claude Debussy. Three favorites by influential modernist: *Prélude à l'Après-midi d'un Faune, Nocturnes,* and *La Mer.* Reprinted from early French editions. 279pp. 9 x 12. 24441-5 Pa. **$14.95**

SYMPHONY IN D MINOR IN FULL SCORE, César Franck. Superb, authoritative edition of Franck's only symphony, an often-performed and recorded masterwork of late French romantic style. 160pp. 9 x 12. 25373-2 Pa. **$11.95**

THE GREAT WALTZES IN FULL SCORE, Johann Strauss, Jr. Complete scores of eight melodic masterpieces: The Beautiful Blue Danube, Emperor Waltz, Tales of the Vienna Woods, Wiener Blut, four more. Authoritative editions. 336pp. 8⅜ x 11¼. 26009-7 Pa. **$14.95**

THE FIREBIRD IN FULL SCORE (Original 1910 Version), Igor Stravinsky. Handsome, inexpensive edition of modern masterpiece, renowned for brilliant orchestration, glowing color. Authoritative Russian edition. 176pp. 9⅜ x 12¼. (Available in U.S. only) 25535-2 Pa. **$10.95**

PETRUSHKA IN FULL SCORE: Original Version, Igor Stravinsky. The definitive full-score edition of Stravinsky's masterful score for the great Ballets Russes 1911 production of *Petrushka.* 160pp. 9⅜ x 12¼. (Available in U.S. only) 25680-4 Pa. **$11.95**

Available from your music dealer or write for
***free** Music Catalog to Dover Publications, Inc., Dept. MUBI,*
31 East 2nd Street, Mineola, N.Y. 11501.